START

Lead Well • **Be Well** • Do Well

**Equip your kids with the mindset and skills they need
to thrive in a highly competitive world**

Laurie Bodine

Well Well Well Press

The following are Trademarks and/or Copyrights of START Leadership:

The Business & Family Organization	WIN Map
The Complete Leader	START Leadership Process
RRR: Leadership Attributes	Essential Leadership Skills

Publisher's Note: This publication is designed to provide information only in regard to the subject matter covered. It is not intended to provide psychological or professional services.

Published by Well Well Well Press, San Francisco, CA

Cover design by Melissa Hutton

Library of Congress/ISBN 9780988359949

Printed in the United States of America

Author's Website: START-Leadership.com

CONTENTS

FOREWORD

Many have described the problems kids face growing up in competitive, college prep communities, including pressure from their parents who are concerned that they may be left behind in an increasingly demanding and uncertain world. What to do, in the face of these challenges, has been less clear. Until now.

Laurie Bodine is a powerful voice of reason and vision. In START, she presents a leadership path to success — and happiness — that works. Not only have I used START successfully in my own family, I have worked to integrate it into the classrooms and families of our school.

We have seen the impact START makes on developing essential leadership skills while building social and emotional capacity and connection. We have used START to unite our parents, teachers, and students with a common leadership language and process to navigate their lives effectively.

By shifting to a leadership mindset and committing to the START approach, you and your kids will reap the benefits now, and in the future.

– Bill Brady, Leadership Director, The Haverford School
   2015

Thanks to my cofounders, John and Jack; to the START Team, Jane, Julie, Jan, and Bill; to the START Champions, Bill, Ron, Joe, Jay, Carla, Amy, Alicia, Patty, Liz, Lee, Beth, Mary, Jim, Pam, Stephanie, and Robin; and to the many parents, students, educators, and professionals who have embraced START for good.

The Secrets of the 10%

"Only 10% of students are prepared to truly succeed, and to be happy and healthy in college and in life. I know who, and I know why, and it's not what you think."

For me, getting a good seatmate on a long flight is like winning the lottery. On a business trip to Washington, DC to speak at an ethics conference, I won big. My seatmate turned out to be a professor from Duke University who was friendly, engaging, and clearly, quite brilliant.

How lucky! I had long harbored the vision of getting my son into an elite school like Duke. And now I had five hours to find out exactly how to do it.

My son was four at the time.

The conversation didn't go quite as I expected. I was looking for an insider's list of to-dos, things I could start early to give my son an edge in admissions. But the professor challenged what I believed — what our generation of parents seems to believe — about raising "successful" kids. That is, raising the kind of kids who can, for example, get into a school like Duke. Or Harvard. Or any of America's "Top Schools."

He told me that in his experience and in that of his colleagues at other selective colleges, only 10% of students are prepared to truly succeed, and to be happy and healthy in college and in life. And he knew their secrets.

"I know who, and I know why, and it's not what you think."

The professor explained:

> "On the first day of freshman English, I give an assignment to write a paper —
> any format, any topic — and to turn it in at the next class so I can get a sense
> of each student's ability. Immediately, hands shoot up. 'How long should it be?
> What should the topic be? Should it be single-spaced or double-spaced? How
> will it be graded?'
>
> I repeat the assignment and confirm that it won't be graded, that I just need to
> gauge their proficiency level so I can tailor the class to meet their needs. But
> they don't believe me; they've been conditioned not to. They line up at office
> hours, desperate for further direction, and when I don't give it to them, they pull
> out their cell phones and call their parents. 'He won't tell me what to do — will
> you talk to him for me?'"

The professor continued:

> "Over my 20 years on the faculty, my colleagues and I around the country have witnessed a progressive decline in student preparedness, initiative, and self-direction. These students are struggling — they're stressed, misguided, and unhappy. They have no idea how to take the lead in their own lives.
>
> But there are always a few — about 10% — who tackle the assignment without further direction. They write their paper and turn it in. Their behavior across the board is strikingly different. That difference is not about grades or test scores or the density of their résumés. It's their approach to life and work — their confidence, their initiative — their willingness to step up and step in. They aren't necessarily the most gifted intellectually, but I've come to discover that these 10% are the ones who have what it takes to succeed and to be happy and healthy — here at Duke, at work, and in life."

The conversation was as disquieting as it was promising. I was stunned. How could it be that 90% of kids on their way to college, in college, and on their way out of college are struggling in such significant ways? How did we get to a place where parents of four-year-olds are planning how to get their kids into a good college, and where so many of us have come to think that this is normal — that we have no other choice?

I was determined to discover everything I could about the secrets of the 10% and how to put them to work.

Once home from the conference, I set to work. As a parent and an executive strategist working at the time for Baxter Healthcare, I began to notice striking similarities between the leadership and management of exceptional businesses and those of exceptional families and classrooms — especially with respect to developing, empowering, and inspiring leaders who can make a positive, productive, and constructive impact.

In what would become a decade of research in the workplace, at universities, on think-tanks, in elementary, middle, and high schools, on playgrounds, and in families, I set out to confirm, use, and then share the secrets of exceptional organizations, families, classrooms, and workplaces — the secrets of the 10% — and how to use them to equip our kids with the mindset and skills they need to navigate and flourish in the high pressure, high stakes culture in which they are growing up and will one day be working.

In the end, despite the widespread and accelerating changes in our increasingly competitive world, the news is good. What my colleagues and I have discovered in the research, including the evidence we're generating in our own field studies, points to an efficient and effective framework that every family can use at home, starting today.

We are not the first to observe, analyze, nor report the implications of our competitive culture on the well-being and performance of our kids. We are also not the first to offer solutions to address the issues prevalent in our college prep communities. A list of those who have pioneered research in this field is included in the bibliography.

What we present in START is a synthesis of the compelling research organized into five straightforward steps that you can use with your family. The START Leadership approach is founded on principles that link leadership, happiness, and success — each of which is essential to be well and do well in today's competitive culture. The relationship of these three elements is important — and it leads us to The Secrets of the 10%.

The Secrets of the 10%

1. Happiness drives success (not the other way around)

   When we are well, we can do well.

2. Leadership drives happiness

   When we develop mastery, autonomy and purpose, we thrive.

3. START drives leadership

   When we practice leadership language and processes, we build essential knowhow for living life well.

These secrets are embedded into the five steps of the START framework. Kids raised with this leadership approach develop the emotional intelligence and intrinsic motivation that fosters initiative, meaningful connection, and engagement at home, at school, and ultimately at work and in life. They have opportunities to discover, tune in to, develop, and align their innate wiring and interests with the needs they discover in their family, school, community, and one day, at work, providing the sense of mastery, autonomy, and purpose that leads to well-being.

What's more, the START Leadership Process is enjoyable. Kids who experience this approach during childhood report greater satisfaction, joy, and hope, even in the midst of working hard and facing challenges. They learn to take the lead in their own lives, using what we call small "l" leadership, and to then take the lead in the pursuit of worthwhile goals, or what we call Big "L" Leadership. In so doing, they develop the attributes of effective leaders — *Responsibility*, *Resilience*, and *Resourcefulness* — that are essential for broad success.

The leadership approach outlined in this book provides a path to happier and healthier kids, giving them structure and space to grow into and live up to their full potential, even in crushingly competitive, college prep communities. It works for kids of all ages — from pre-K through college. And it's never too early or too late to begin.

In Part One, *The START Leadership Approach*, you'll find a discussion of a central challenge families face today, the case for leadership, and the definitions and processes that set the stage for implementation of the START solution.

In Part Two, *START Leadership in Action*, you'll find the five-step action plan you can use — starting today — to equip your kids with the mindset and skills they need to thrive now and in a future that's changing too rapidly to predict.

We're in the midst of a leadership crisis — a crisis that executives and educators rank as a top concern. More urgently, our kids are struggling — yet they have no platform or power to resolve this alone. We, as parents, teachers, community leaders, and professionals, have the opportunity to step into the gap, to provide solutions, and to turn this situation around for our kids and for their future.

We can't wait for our schools, colleges, businesses and communities to shift. We must start at home, in our own families. We must encourage and foster our kids' well-being while modeling, teaching, and reinforcing the leadership mindset and skills that will prepare them to navigate and thrive in the face of rising challenges.

By providing the tools and the opportunities for our kids to take the lead in their own lives, we will equip them with exactly what they need to be well and do well in a highly competitive world. And in the process, we have the collective potential to shift the culture in our schools, communities, and businesses for good.

Let's START now.

Note: START at Work

Individual professionals as well as teams, departments, divisions, and companies around the country use the START Leadership framework to drive alignment, engagement, satisfaction, and results in the workplace. Because the principles of START are founded on universal leadership principles, they work at work *and* at home.

As you read through the principles outlined here, consider the ways in which you could use them in the workplace, integrating your personal and professional approach, to drive effectiveness and well-being.

PART ONE

The START Leadership Approach

The Challenge for Families

Think for a minute — what is it you want most for your kids?

In the decade I've been asking this question of parents around the country — those with kids in private, public, and faith-based schools — most parents tell me that what they want is for their kids to be *happy*.

Then they quickly add — and *healthy*. And then, as if it goes without saying, they add *and to live up to their potential*.

But herein lies the rub. The current path to "living up to potential" in our high pressure, high stakes, college prep culture actually interferes with happiness and health. There's a gap — a disconnect — between what we *believe* is most important, happy and healthy, and how we behave — what we say and do — day to day. And it's prevalent in every college prep community in the country. The challenge for families is how to achieve *all three*: happy, healthy, and living up to potential.

The push for our kids to
be all and do all
interferes with their ability to
be well and do well.

In the current environment, despite the belief that raising happy and healthy kids is most important, highly involved parents have been implicated in prioritizing and micromanaging performance and achievement above all else. Why? Because the competition is fierce, and college admissions are at stake. And everyone is watching.

As the most educated and affluent generation of parents anywhere, at any time, we're prepared to do whatever it takes to help them succeed and be happy. Our fear? That our kids may be seen as ordinary, that they may be left out, or worse, left behind. And if they are, we fear that it may be our fault — because we didn't do enough.

But virtually every expert in the country says that with this approach, this push to perform and achieve, along with our offers to help, we are ensuring that our kids will be neither successful nor happy. Stress, distress, and anxiety are up, yet preparedness for college, work, and life is down.

Even in families who don't push, kids are negatively impacted by the stress and pressure that comes from the prevailing culture in their school and community — and from their peers.

Leadership offers a solution.

The Value of a Leadership Mindset

Leadership tends to be defined narrowly, if we think to define it at all. But in fact, leadership, in the way it is defined most recently in research, academia, and business is broad, inclusive, and nuanced — and it starts with taking the lead in one's own life.

Whether done well or poorly, the way our family functions provides the first, most powerful model of leadership that our kids experience. We have the opportunity to be intentional about the way we lead, and about the way we teach and reinforce leadership skills in our family.

Forward-thinking families can choose to define and articulate the definitions and behaviors of leadership in an affirmative, productive, and constructive way — and to create a family culture that provides opportunities for each family member to learn to take the lead.

The Family Organization

One intriguing way to envision the ways in which leadership shows up in the family is to consider the parallels it has with those in other organizations, such as the workplace. The similarities are striking, given that the dynamics in organizations, large and small, are based on the social, biological, and psychological sciences that govern all human actions and interactions. They also dovetail nicely with the stages of child development, especially with respect to the pursuit of mastery, autonomy, and purpose.

In our primary research, we have shown that this framework provides a foundation that can be used productively at home to optimize individual interactions and family dynamics.

Once established, the mindset and skills develop with increasing sophistication. Kids can apply their knowledge and experiences from home to social interactions and to their work in the classroom, in college, and ultimately, in life and work.

The Business and Family Organization

Business	Family	Purpose/Management Goals
CEO/Executive Team	Mom and Dad	Provide vision, leadership, and direction; strategic and tactical planning, financial management, personnel development; establish the culture.
Entry Level Employees	Young Kids (0-6)	Need management oversight; purpose is to learn basic position requirements (including safety, health, manners).
Management Trainees	Elementary Age (6-12)	Able to work independently with lessening management oversight; purpose is to learn self-direction and pre-management skills.
Managers & Directors	Middle & High School Age (12–18)	Able to manage a variety of activities; can assist in the management of entry level team members (including younger siblings); purpose is to develop and demonstrate skills in time and project management, negotiation, and planning skills.
Vice President	College Age	Responsible for high-level decision making in all areas of responsibility (school, room, board, part-time job, extracurriculars); purpose is to master life management and to align innate wiring and true interests to professional and personal opportunities.
President	Young Adults	Responsible for creating own vision, strategy, goals and objectives.
CEO/ Executive Team	Mom and Dad	The cycle begins again.
Advisory Board	Grandparents	Experienced and respected advisors providing support, guidance; invited position.

Small "l" and Big "L" Leadership

The language of leadership that START uses with families and schools is simple and can be understood by even the youngest kids. When we introduce and consistently use leadership language, we provide the environment, tools, and context that kids need to frame the choices they make and the actions they take on a daily basis.

We define leadership from both a small "l" leadership and Big "L" Leadership perspective.

Small "l" leadership is the day-to-day leadership that kids with initiative demonstrate when they take actions that have positive and productive outcomes. Over time, kids practicing small "l" leadership become effective leaders in their own lives and go on to make a difference in their families, school, and community, and eventually, in the workplace.

Examples of small "l" leadership:

- Preschool: Getting ready for bed without help or reminders — by brushing teeth, putting on PJs, putting dirty clothes in the hamper, picking out a book, and climbing into bed.

- Elementary school: Getting ready for school on time and without reminders by getting up with an alarm, getting dressed, eating breakfast, packing lunches and backpacks.

- High school: Completing school work independently, keeping track of their own things, such as a cell phone or house key, doing household chores, and assisting others when they see a need.

- At all ages: Holding the door for someone; picking up trash found on the sidewalk; choosing not to cheat; helping a younger child on the playground; voting in school or civic elections.

Big "L" Leadership is the goal-directed leadership that kids demonstrate when they work with others to achieve worthwhile goals at school, home, and in their communities. It's about understanding what needs to be done, why their participation is important, and how to mobilize themselves and others to do it.

Examples of Big "L" Leadership:

- Preschool: Helping the family with simple chores such as dusting tables, putting toys away, raking leaves.

- Elementary school: Organizing an activity at home or school such as a food drive with classmates or a weekend activity for the family.

- Middle school: Planning and organizing activities that serve others such as volunteering as student peer advisors or visiting and reading to the elderly.

- High school: Engaging in a mission-driven organization as a founder, officer, or member; starting a part-time dog walking or baby-sitting business with friends.

Small "l" leadership: Leading Self

Make decisions and take actions that have positive and productive outcomes.

Big "L" Leadership: Leading Others

Mobilize self and others in pursuit of worthwhile goals.

The Complete Leader

Leadership takes many forms. We've developed a simplified model that represents four primary styles used by effective leaders in a wide range of successful organizations. Each of these styles can be used by parents at home to model and teach leadership and to reinforce the development of leadership skills in their kids.

A Complete Leader is adept at identifying the appropriate leadership style in any situation to achieve the best short-term and long-term results — at work or at home. By using these leadership styles appropriately and with consistency, parents create a culture that enables their kids to learn and master these styles and to use them effectively to take the lead in their own lives and work.

The four styles of the Complete Leader represent a continuum from most to least involvement and direction by the leader. The four leadership styles are Command, Coach, Collaborate, and Champion. The following diagram includes examples of how to use each style.

Complete Leadership Styles

The Complete Leader: Skilled and experienced in the appropriate use of each style to maximize effectiveness.

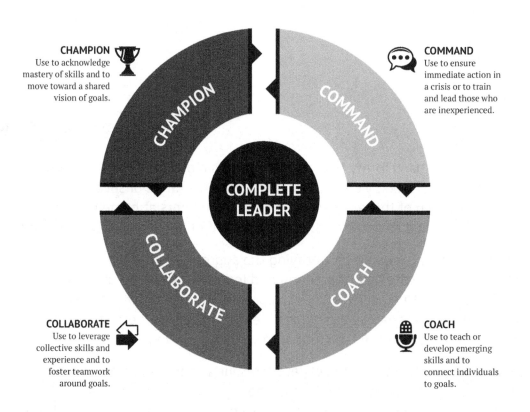

CHAMPION
Use to acknowledge mastery of skills and to move toward a shared vision of goals.

COMMAND
Use to ensure immediate action in a crisis or to train and lead those who are inexperienced.

COLLABORATE
Use to leverage collective skills and experience and to foster teamwork around goals.

COACH
Use to teach or develop emerging skills and to connect individuals to goals.

The EQ Advantage

Leadership effectiveness has been shown to correlate with another key factor. In addition to the structural elements of the Complete Leader Styles, it is also important to consider the impact that managing one's emotions and the emotional environment have on the development of our kids' (and our own) ability to lead well, be well, and do well.

Daniel Goleman's ground-breaking work on Emotional Intelligence (known as EI or EQ) shows that in the workplace, EQ is the single best predictor of leadership effectiveness. IQ is far less predictive of workplace success than EQ. Goleman's research has shown that 70% of the time, it is not the smartest person (high IQ) in the room that is the best leader, but rather the person who can effectively manage their own emotions and respond effectively to the emotional state of others (high EQ).

EQ is the single best predictor of effective leadership.

70% of the time, EQ trumps IQ in predicting workplace success.

Why is this? Neurological research shows that our brains are hard wired to prioritize emotions over rational thought. Because of this, unexpected or strong emotions can hijack our rational thinking. It happens to all of us. Think for a minute about a time this has happened to you and to your kids. Adults and kids who can recognize and then manage emotions are more effective in responding rationally to input, making sound decisions, and achieving productive outcomes. When we model, teach, and reinforce this for our kids, they're better able to build their EQ as well.

Strengthening awareness and raising our own and our kids' EQ can be accomplished through the investment of time and effort in four key areas. In a wide range of situations, this investment helps us all to act and interact more effectively. Modeling and teaching the importance of EQ, along with the strategies to build it, reinforces the development of EQ in our kids.

The four areas of EQ mastery include two in knowledge: Self-Awareness and Social Awareness, and two in behavior: Self-Management and Relationship Management.

Self-Awareness means knowing one's emotional and social profile, including strengths, communication style, triggers, and preferences.

Effective **Self-Management** results from applying one's Self-Awareness to manage one's environment and behaviors to be at one's best. This includes controlling impulses, getting enough sleep, scheduling enough time.

Social Awareness takes the form of knowing that others with whom you live, learn, and work also have an emotional and social profile that may be similar or different than yours.

Effective **Relationship Management** results from applying one's Social Awareness to constructively manage one's interactions with others.

The WIN Map

In order to build the EQ and connections that foster leading well, being well, and doing well, it is essential for our kids to be given time, space and guidance as they:

- Tune in to how they're innately **W**ired — the natural strengths, talents, and skills they use to approach situations and people around them,

- Tune in to their emerging **I**nterests — identify the things that they like, like to do, and/or care about, and

- Tune in to the **N**eeds they discover in their world: family, school, and community.

This is true for us too — personally and professionally. When we align what we're good at with what we like and apply both to meet needs around us, we're at our best. When kids use their innate Wiring to meet the Needs in areas that are of Interest to them, they can engage and excel naturally as well. In this process, kids experience a connection to the purpose of their work that sustains motivation and engagement and allows them to map their path through college, major and career selection.

The WIN Map

Individual Discovery and Connection

WIRED
What I'm Naturally
Good At

INTERESTS
What I Like

NEEDS
Opportunities I See
in the World

 = **Your Path**

We can start this process by modeling the WIN approach for our kids. We can assess our own Wiring and Interests and the way we apply them to meet the Needs of our family, community, and workplace. We can then develop narratives to share our stories about searching for and finding our paths and how we apply our wiring and interests to contribute to needs as parents, as professionals, as volunteers.

At home, it is possible to create opportunities for our kids to discover and experience their own WIN Maps, along with the WIN Maps of their siblings, and to discover how they can collaborate to optimize experience and maximize outcomes. Supporting our kids in developing WIN Maps to reflect their development in the various communities in which they participate over time lays the groundwork for making important decisions throughout life.

Tools to further assess the ways in which your kids (and you) are innately wired are available through Gallup StrengthsFinder, Myers Briggs, and others. Wiring resource links are listed in the Bibliography.

Steps to WIN

First, complete your own WIN Map(s).

Then, assist your kids in completing their WIN Map(s).

Create narratives, or stories to share your WIN Map(s).

Refine and repeat as appropriate, over time.

The START Leadership Process

The secrets of exceptional organizations, families, classrooms, and individuals are grounded in the social, biological, and psychological sciences as they relate to happiness and success. In our research, we've identified a leadership mindset and approach that provides a direct and efficient path to attaining both. We've organized the five essential leadership practices into an effective leadership framework: The START Leadership Process. START provides a five-step action plan to put the secrets to work in your family.

The START process is as effective for professionals as it is for parents, teachers, and students. START is in use in innovative and traditional organizations as well as in select schools across the country. In addition to the benefits for kids, when parents integrate this leadership approach into their lives both personally and professionally, well-being, engagement and effectiveness go up for them too — at home, at work, and in the community. START provides professional development for both sides of the work-life equation, creating greater integration and peace of mind for those who use it. And one day, your kids will put their leadership skills to work at work.

At home, the START framework provides the process, language, and tools to align your family's Strategy – values, goals, and strategic vision with your Tactics – the few activities you prioritize and select to achieve your Strategy. Periodic Assessment of your Strategy and Tactics ensures you stay on track over time. Routines anchor the daily work and activities each member of your family does and that you do together in order to achieve your Tactics. Training formalizes opportunities for your kids to discover, practice, and develop essential life and leadership skills through the daily experience of living their lives while maximizing their opportunities and solving their own problems.

START Leadership Process

STRATEGY	*Strategic vision, values, and goals*
TACTICS	*Tactics to achieve the strategy*
ASSESSMENT	*Assessment to stay on track*
ROUTINES	*Routines link daily work to tactics*
TRAINING	*Training to develop essential skills*

PART TWO

START Leadership in Action

Step 1: Strategy

What you want for your family

strat·e·gy (noun): a careful plan or method for achieving
a particular goal, usually over a long period of time

As you read this chapter, consider:

1. What you want for yourself, your family, and your relationships. What are your goals for your kids when they leave for college, begin their first job, and start their own family? How do you hope they'll be prepared to handle success and to face disappointment, setbacks, and loss?

2. The importance of having a family Strategy and engaging your kids in developing the strategic goals and values that will help everyone in the family to lead well, be well, and do well.

Overview

A family Strategy, informed by your values, acts as a guide for your family's actions and the decisions you make on a daily, monthly, and yearly basis in order to accomplish those goals and long-term vision.

Your Strategy provides the meaningful link between your goals and the decisions and actions you take, providing a reliable sense of structure and purpose for kids. Without a strategy, decisions and actions can appear as arbitrary reactions to events and situations, which can be unsettling to kids.

Your use of a family Strategy also serves as a model to teach and reinforce essential leadership experiences, including strategic thinking, critical thinking, and decision making to build knowledge and skills in your kids.

It's essential to include your kids in the development of your family Strategy and to communicate the importance it has in guiding your family's actions and decisions. It's also important to model the commitment you are making by using it to guide the family's decisions and actions.

Developing a Family Strategy

1. Select Your Family Values

Over several days or weeks, identify, define, and discuss the things you value most as a family. Take as much time as you need to make it meaningful. Invite each family member, over the age of five, to participate in the process.

Use this values list (or the Values Cards with definitions in the START Family Leadership Kit) to prompt discussion. Include additional values that are not listed that you and your family think are important.

Kindness	Integrity	Adventure	Tolerance	Family
Faith	Loyalty	Fun	Courage	Individuality
Hope	Respect	Learning	Work Ethic	_____
Joy	Service	Teamwork	Perseverance	_____

There are no right or wrong answers. The process of seeking, considering, and respecting the input of each family member is as important, if not more important, than the specific values you select. In this process, you are modeling, teaching and reinforcing a leadership mindset, process, and skill by respecting and valuing the contribution of each family member.

   a. Invite each family member to select four to five core values that they feel are most important.

   b. Together, take turns presenting and discussing the values that are most important to each family member.

   c. The five values that receive the most votes become the family's core values. Note: If any family member feels strongly about the importance of a value that is not selected, invite them to select it as an additional personal value.

2. Select Your Family's Goals

Identify and select the three or four goals that are most important to your family. Strongly consider including the goal to develop the leadership attributes of Responsibility, Resilience, and Resourcefulness. Use the definitions below to prompt discussion. Include additional goals you and your family consider to be important.

Responsible   I know what to do, and
I step up to do it.

Resilient   I know why I am the one to do it, and
I stay with it, even when it is hard.

Resourceful   I know how to do it, modeling creativity, and
I know how to work with others to get it done, modeling collaboration.

3. Draft Your Family Strategy

Draft a short statement that reflects your selected values, goals, and vision for your family. Use the template below to facilitate your process.

In the_____ (insert last name) family, we value
_____ ,_____ ,_____ ,_____ ,_____ (list values),

and we choose activities and actions that support the development of
_____ ,_____ ,_____ (list goals),

in order to develop as individuals who can
lead well, be well, and do well, now and in the future.

Commit to supporting this Strategy in your family.

Family Strategy Example

An example of my family's Strategy, including values, goals, and the resulting strategic vision, looks like this:

In the Bodine Family, we value
Kindness, Courage, Learning, Service, and Fun

and we choose activities and actions that support the development of
Responsibility, Resilience, and Resourcefulness

in order to develop as individuals who can
lead well, be well, and do well, now and in the future.

Strategy Case Study: Engaging the Family

A family new to START, with kids in middle school and high school, found that introducing this leadership approach was a little awkward at first, but with perseverance and a commitment to the whole process, they succeeded.

The well-intentioned but extremely busy parents had been using a Command style of leadership with their kids. During family discussions, when the kids failed to respond as expected, it was typical for their Dad to take the floor and raise his voice (Command) until he gained compliance.

When Dad initiated a conversation to introduce the family to the idea of developing a family Strategy together, there were some raised eyebrows among the kids. They were suspicious that this might be yet another attempt to get them to do what their parents wanted.

Rather than stay to discuss it, the kids claimed they had so much work to do they couldn't stay and dashed off to do family chores, homework, and walk the dog without being nagged – atypical behavior for the family.

While pleased the kids were showing Responsibility in doing their work, Mom and Dad acknowledged that the kids were using any excuse, even chores and homework, to avoid confrontation.

Mom and Dad tried again a few days later. Over several weeks of fits and starts, the kids came to trust that their parents were sincere in soliciting their input for the good of the family and its members. The kids sensed a shift in their parents' mindset, and noticed they backed it up with a shift in behavior. Most obvious, the Commanding style of their Dad had been replaced with Collaboration.

Instead of discussions of homework, grades, goals scored, and chores — the previously dominant conversational topics in the family — conversations about values and interests became the new norm. These exchanges proved to be some of the most authentic and meaningful they'd had. The kids showed up before dinner and stayed at the table long after the meal was finished — to hang out, to laugh, and talk about things that were important to them. They put their phones away. They discussed how people treated each other at school, and how they wanted to treat each other at home. Interests and dreams were examined and their goals emerged.

With input from all, they drafted a family Strategy with values and goals they all agreed to support.

Step 2: **Tactics**

How to align what you want with what you do

tac·tic (noun): actions carefully planned to achieve a specific end

As you read this step, consider:

1. How you'll support your kids in selecting activities that align with the family Strategy, their WIN Map, and your available family resources of time, attention, and money.

2. Which of your actions and interactions with your kids build their belief in themselves as Responsible, Resilient, and Resourceful and which actions diminish it?

Overview

With your family Strategy in mind, the second step in the process is to select the few Tactical activities that best support the family's Strategy, and over time, to phase out those activities that do not support it.

Every action, interaction, and activity involving your kids has a positive, neutral, or negative impact on their belief in themselves as Responsible, Resilient, and Resourceful — from daily conversations about planning and behavior to chores, homework, and extracurriculars. Taking care to ensure these actions and interactions build your kids' belief in themselves has a tremendously positive, long-term impact on happiness and success.

The spacing, scheduling and number of activities also impacts our kids' abilities to lead well, be well, and do well. There's precious little time left after school, homework, and sleep to participate in anything else, yet we face a constant demand to add activities — sports, music, tutors, community service, clubs. In a culture where every day we're made to feel as though our kids may be left out or left behind, it's challenging to know best how to proceed. Lack of sleep, distress, and cognitive overload all have a significant, negative impact on mood, memory, and performance.

An effective approach is to use the Tactics Decision Tree on page 63 to identify and select your Tactics, and then take action to implement your decisions in daily family life.

Selecting Your Tactics

Use your family's Strategy, WIN Maps, and Resources as a guide to align and select each of your family members' Tactical activities.

1. List Your Current Tactics

List all the Tactical activities in which each family member participates or wants to participate on Post-It notes — one activity per Post-It.

Include sleep, down time, free time, school, homework, chores, extracurricular, personal, and family activities.

2. Align Your Tactics

For each member of the family and for the family as a whole, align activities with the family's Strategy — vision, values, and goals, your kids' WIN Maps — wiring, interests, and needs, and with available Resources — time, attention, and money.

Use the Tactics Decision Tree tool to facilitate the process, placing the Post-It for each activity in the appropriate category: continue current activities that are in alignment, phase in activities for which you have a value or goal that has no current activity, phase out current activities that do not align, and do not add new activities that do not align.

Repeat the exercise as necessary until you are able to reduce the number of remaining activities to optimize sleep, reduce stress levels, and lessen cognitive load.

Tactics Decision Tree

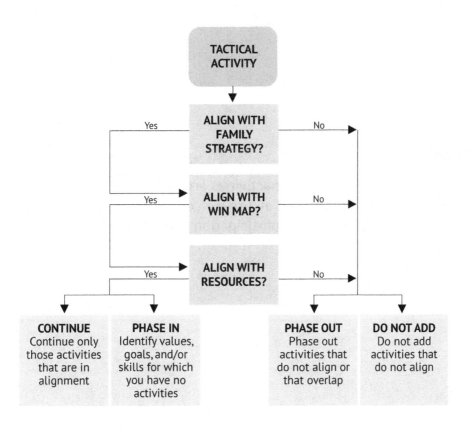

3. Implement

Take action to phase in or phase out activities according to your alignment process. In some cases, waiting until the end of a season or the completion of a commitment may be necessary. In others, ending participation immediately may be possible.

Family Tactics Example

Using the steps in the Tactics Decision Tree, my husband and I made the Tactical decisions for the family when our kids were very young. As they got older, we expanded the decision making for family activities to include everyone's input and increased the sophistication of the process over time.

Example of our family's Tactics, aligned with our Values, our WIN Maps, and our Resources, include:

Kindness

> Activity: At least one meal together each day of the week during which we actively and compassionately listen to one another share the best and most challenging parts of our day

> Benefits: Builds Resilience and Resourcefulness through compassion, connection, emotional intelligence, communication skills, and strategic thinking

Courage

> Activity: Trying at least one new thing a year, even when it means we might be bad at it before we learn if we will enjoy it or if we will be good at it

> Benefits: Builds Resilience and a growth mindset, prioritizes engagement over perfection, introduces a path to overcoming the limitations of fear

Learning

> Activities: Games and reading during the week (TV only on weekends), museums in cities we visit, NPR on the car radio, books on tape

> Benefits: Builds Responsibility, Resilience, and Resourcefulness by reinforcing the value of learning as a lifelong, enjoyable endeavor that can be woven into the fabric of daily life

Service

> Activities: Community volunteering, pro bono clients, mentoring

> Benefits: Builds Responsibility, Resilience and Resourcefulness. A focus on others demonstrates connection to community and provides a real-life experience that we each have value, that we matter

Fun

> Activities: Weekly game night, family adventures, vacations, family movies (*Muppet Treasure Island* – still the family favorite)

> Benefits: Builds Resilience and connection, joy, and a sense of adventure while reinforcing the importance of well-being

Tactics Case Study: Reading Between the Lines

The parents in a family participating in the Parent Leadership Labs in a START school shared this story about their ten-year-old son, who was also participating in a START Leadership-in-Action Initiative with his class:

> "We were using the Tactics Decision Tree with our kids, to be sure their activities aligned with our family Strategy, our WIN Maps, and our resources. Conner had listed his many activities on Post-It notes and was sorting them into piles of those that aligned and those that did not align with his Wiring and Interests.
>
> When he got to his note for basketball, he hovered over the 'No: Phase Out' pile. He looked up to see that we were watching and quickly shifted the Post-It to "Yes: Continue" pile. We didn't know what to make of it so we asked, 'Are you less interested in basketball this year?' He summoned his courage to tell us that, although he had really liked it when he was younger, he was playing now because he thought we wanted him to. We had both played basketball. He feared that if he quit, he would disappoint us, but he felt overwhelmed with

the step up in fifth grade homework on top of all his activities. He's a great swimmer, and he loves it. He told us he'd rather focus on swimming and have some free time to play pick-up basketball with his friends.

When we told him we totally supported his decision, the relief on his face was apparent. How had we missed it? He had seemed more stressed this year, but we weren't sure why. He talked with his coach about the challenge of completing his school work, and was able to phase out as the season ended. HIs disposition brightened almost immediately. He's getting more sleep and now has scheduled down time three days a week. He's been calmer and more able to focus on his school work. He's kinder to his sister. And his conversations with us have been more open and honest."

Step 3: Assessment

How to stay on track over time

as·sess·ment (noun): the act of making a judgment about something

As you read this step, consider:

1. As your kids grow and develop, consider whether their actions, interactions, and activities continue to align with the family Strategy, WIN Map, and Resources.

2. The responsibilities and privileges your kids have now and those that may be appropriate for them to add in the coming months or year.

Overview

The third step in the process, Assessment, ensures that our Tactics continue to align with our Strategy by periodically taking stock of where things stand. Life gets more demanding, with increasing challenges and more opportunities to participate in activities every year. Kids also mature, their interests and abilities change, and they make new friends. Adding activities comes more easily to them (and us) than subtracting. Without assessing where we are several times each year, we're at risk of over-scheduling and of missing the opportunities to acknowledge the subtle but significant growth our kids are demonstrating.

At every developmental stage, we are assessing our kids and our kids are assessing us.

We ask:

> "Are we still on track? Are you developing in the ways that are normal for your age? Do all the activities and behaviors carried over from last season or last year still support our family values and goals? Do they reflect your wiring and interests? Do we have the resources — including time, attention, and money — to support them all? Are there any that are missing?"

Our kids ask:

> "Can I trust you to support me in reaching my goals, to be consistent, to have my best interests at heart — not your interests disguised as my interests, i.e. if I get good grades, make the travel team, play first chair, you will be a successful parent and look good to your friends? Can I trust you to see me as capable and to nudge me forward, even when I'm reluctant?"

Families benefit most when Assessment occurs several times throughout the year. School breaks, birthdays, the start of the school year, or the start of the new year are ideal for scheduling check-ins. Also important are the Assessments that occur on an as-needed basis, when prospective activities are introduced or current demands become too stressful.

Scheduling time to Assess whether or not you're all on track demonstrates the importance of the activity, and in so doing parents model, teach, and reinforce an essential life and leadership skill.

To stay on track over time, it is important to take time to assess whether or not current activities still align with: 1) the values and goals of the family Strategy, 2) each of your family member's WIN maps, and 3) available resources of time, attention, and money. It is also important to assess the alignment of responsibilities and earned privileges.

Assessing the alignment between responsibility and privileges during this process can offer great value to the development of essential life and leadership skills. At each development phase, your kids are able to take on more responsibility and earn more privileges, and we, as parents, can support our kids by monitoring both at each developmental stage. Sometimes, our kids are ready for more responsibility and privilege before we realize it. They may be ready to dress themselves, do homework on their own, choose their own activities, stay home alone, or go out with friends alone before we recognize it. Routinely assessing readiness helps in this alignment process.

Other times, we may expand responsibilities and privileges beyond what our kids are ready for and things don't go as expected, and/or they are not able to keep their agreements. When we can talk with them, without shame, about the fact that we may have expanded too far for the moment and that pulling back for a time may be the best course, we teach and reinforce our belief in their ability to learn and develop responsibility in line with privilege.

Assessing Alignment and Progress

1. Schedule Assessment Dates

Schedule two to three times during the year to formally assess alignment.

The start of summer or winter breaks, birthdays, and the new year are possible options.

Date 1:_____ Date 2:_____ Date 3:_____

Be on the lookout for informal opportunities that arise throughout the year to assess alignment.

2. (Re) Align Your Tactics

Using the Tactics Decision Tree, complete the assessment of old and new activities.

- How well does each activity align with values and goals, wiring and interests, and available resources?

- Have family member's wiring or interests changed? Do they still enjoy each of their activities? What are they getting out of it — are they learning something, connecting with friends, having fun?

- Are there other activities they might prefer to do instead of one or more that they're doing now?

- Develop exit plans to phase out activities that no longer align, and phase in activities that may be missing.

3. Acknowledge Progress

Acknowledge growth in the level of responsibility each of your kids has demonstrated since the last assessment. Invite them to share their assessment of themselves. Note areas where there is room for continued improvement.

In line with growing levels of responsibility, identify additional privileges they have earned as well as several stretch goals to add for the next assessment period.

Family Assessment Example

In the sixth grade, the son of a START family wanted to use his birthday money to buy a video game console to play sports games. Before doing so, his parents asked him to Assess the decision using the Tactics Decision Tree — paying particular attention to the implications video game playing could have on his well-being, including brain development.

In the research he did, he was surprised to learn that more than one to two hours per day of screen time caused structural and functional changes in the brain that interfered with emotional control and executive functioning — attention, decision making, and cognitive control. Aligned with his family's Tactic of enjoying screen-free activities during the week, he proposed that he limit his screen time to two hours on the weekend. Given that his weekend schedule was already full, he decided to substitute two hours of weekend television/screen time for two hours of weekend game time.

The assessment process applies to parents as well. In the waiting room of a doctor's office years ago, one of our START moms informally assessed the factors that could be contributing to her declining health. Not only was her energy level low, she was becoming more and more susceptible to viruses and infections. In addition to being a wife, mother, daughter, and friend, co-managing the household, and working full time, she was also volunteering regularly at school and serving as a board member for the county children's shelter.

Although each of these activities aligned with her family's Strategy and with her WIN Map, doing them all did not align with her resource of time. She decided to phase out her advisory board involvement and to significantly reduce her school volunteer time immediately.

The breathing room these decisions made improved both her physical and mental health, and improved her ability to engage in positive and productive ways in all the other areas of her life.

Assessment Case Study: Staying on Track

A mother of a ten-year-old shared an informal assessment experience she had when she got an email from her son's school informing her that he had missed an assignment that day.

> "It was 11:00 at night. I got a ding alerting me to a new email. It was from the school's communication system, informing me that my son, Cole, hadn't turned in his science homework that day. It was not like him to miss an assignment. I was so upset, I was halfway down the hall to his room with plans to wake him up to 'talk' about it when I caught myself and asked 'What would the Leadership approach be in this case?'

> One of the goals in our family Strategy is to raise kids who are responsible for and capable of solving their own problems. So I went back to bed.

At breakfast the next morning, I asked Cole how things were going for him. Did he feel he had enough time to get his school work done on top of karate, Boy Scouts, and lacrosse? The stress and anxiety I could see on his face broke my heart. The story came pouring out — that he had failed to finish his science homework and that he didn't want to go to school. He felt sick and overwhelmed.

We talked about how much he had going on and how he felt about dropping one of his activities. He blurted out karate — and shared that he'd wanted to quit, now that he was playing a team sport that he loved, but didn't want to let down his instructor. I let him know how much I admired his consideration for his teacher, but that making choices according to what we think others want can sometimes cause us to make decisions that aren't healthy for us. He decided to schedule time with his instructor before his next lesson to discuss his decision to leave.

I asked how he might handle the situation of the missed homework with his teacher. He brainstormed a few ideas, and with me acting as a sounding board, he decided to meet with his teacher before class to apologize and to let her know he would be turning in the assignment the next day. He also decided to share his decision to drop one of his activities so that it wouldn't happen again.

On the drive home later that day, he was excited to tell me that the conversation had gone great! His teacher offered to give him half credit for the late assignment along with an opportunity to do some extra credit work to make up the difference. He and I agreed to check in regularly — to be sure he was staying on track and to prevent things from becoming so overwhelming again."

Step 4: **R**outines

How to link daily work to Tactics

rou·tine (noun): a sequence of actions regularly followed

As you read this step, consider:

1. The work you may be doing for your kids that they are capable of doing themselves, and the ways in which you can plan for and transfer responsibility for their work to them.

2. Whether the things you say and do each day align with your Strategy, and how establishing Routines for yourself may reinforce alignment.

Overview

Establishing routines, the fourth step, provides an opportunity to link what each family member does and says every day to Strategy and Tactics.

When kids are learning to walk and talk, we model, teach, and then reinforce the learning of these foundational skills. Once they are well on their way to mastering them, we are proud to let our kids do this work on their own. But as they get older, doing chores, homework, or getting ready for school or practice, we tend to repeat the same reminders and instructions every day. Kids often resist, we escalate, and the cycle repeats. And when we're in a hurry because we either have more to do than we have time to do it, or we haven't managed our time well, the situation can be even more frustrating for everyone.

If instead, we work with our kids to organize the to-dos into a Routine, a repeatable set of actions that occur regularly, we can give our kids a sense of ownership, responsibility, and mastery.

At work, in marketing, manufacturing, finance and such, these are known as "processes." Pilots, during pre-flight preparations and surgeons, in the operating room, use checklists to ensure consistency and quality.

This works at home too. When we link routine, daily activities to our family vision and goals, we connect why the work is important and why taking ownership of the work is important.

Establishing Routines allows for the natural transfer of responsibility for work from parents to kids while strengthening kids' autonomy, mastery, and purpose as they learn to do their work well.

Routines also strengthen kids' abilities to see the emerging patterns in daily life — a skill that will allow them to navigate and manage their lives with greater skill and dexterity.

Throughout the transfer process, kids develop a framework and language with which to interpret and articulate their experiences.

The process supports the development of a growth mindset (we can improve when we try), over a fixed mindset (our ability is fixed regardless of effort).

In this process, we also demonstrate our confidence in our kids' expanding and developing capabilities over time. When we help them see the ways they can transfer the skills they have mastered in one area to another new and potentially challenging area, kids' confidence in their own capability expands.

And finally, proactively managing daily activities with Routines, we reserve our available capacity to respond to the inevitable emergencies that occur in life.

Establishing Routines

1. Capability Assessment

- Evaluate each of your kids' daily activities according to their ability to complete them on their own.

- Consider the current dynamics and patterns of interaction between you and your kids with respect to reminders and help.

- Use the following chart to facilitate the process. Check the boxes that reflect their ability and your patterns.

Kid's Work & Responsibilities	Able: Yes No	With no reminders	With one reminder	With many reminders	With help throughout
Ready for School					
Homework					
Practice / Rehearsal					
Ready for Bed					
Chores					
Other					

2. Establish Routines for All Daily Activities

In cases where you are providing reminders and/or help to your kids for work they are capable of completing on their own, use Routines to transfer responsibility for the work to them.

- Identify the activities for which your kids have the skills and ability to complete work without reminders or help.

- Discuss the importance of transferring responsibilities to accomplish the goals and vision of the family Strategy.

- Co-develop or support your kids in developing a Routine checklist for each activity.

3. Transfer Responsibility

Transfer responsibility using the following options:

- Transfer responsibility immediately for those activities for which your kids have the required mindset and skills.

- If support is needed, co-develop a step-by-step transition plan — who will do what over what period of time — and then transfer responsibility.

- If skills are lacking, complete additional skill development (see Step 5: Training), co-develop a step-by-step transition plan, and then transfer responsibility.

Family Routines Example

In middle school, the weekday "Ready for Bed" routine at our house looked like this:

- ❐ Check planner - pack backpack/gear bag
- ❐ Check lunch schedule – take or buy
- ❐ If take, make lunch
- ❐ Walk the dog
- ❐ Screens (for homework) off by 9:00
- ❐ Phone on the charger
- ❐ Brush teeth and shower
- ❐ Reading in bed by 9:30

Routines Case Study: Getting Dressed

I had this conversation with a friend whose daughter was in the first grade. He was hearing about our approach for the first time.

"How can I use this leadership approach to help me get my six-year-old dressed in the morning? We battle every day about what she's going to wear."

I asked, "What is your goal for your daughter in terms of getting dressed when she goes off to college? Who will be choosing what she wears?"

"Well," he laughed, "I certainly hope she will be able to get herself dressed appropriately by then."

"When do you suppose you'll stop making the decisions for her? At six, you know she's capable of getting dressed on her own, and once she has a Routine and some guidelines, she'll be capable of making appropriate choices. She's likely arguing with you because she knows she's capable, and she wants to do it herself."

Before I finished the sentence, he understood. "I've been making decisions for her that she can make for herself — that's why she's resisting and rebelling. She wants to do it herself."

We talked over how he and his wife would convey their confidence in their daughter's ability, and transfer the responsibility for getting dressed to her. The plan was to start with a direct discussion at the dinner table, including an apology for not recognizing her capability sooner and an acknowledgement of his role in the arguments. They would ask for her thoughts and input, and then work with her to organize her closet and drawers in sections for school, play, and special occasion clothes (Coaching leadership style). And then after a brief transition period (Collaboration leadership style), they would step back and let her take over the routine of selecting the clothes appropriate for the occasion.

Just a few days later, he reported good news. "When we started the discussion, she dashed from the dinner table to her room to start reorganizing her closet — before we'd even finished the conversation. We had fun setting up her closet and dresser drawers. She's so excited and proud to be making these decisions herself. We made a calendar together. She checks each night before bed so she can lay out what she'll wear the next day. We've not had one argument since. Now, instead of arguing, we're reinforcing how responsible and capable she is (Championing leadership style) in doing her own work."

Over the next few weeks, he reported that they had successfully added Routines for getting ready for bed, getting ready for school, and setting the dinner table.

Step 5: Training

How to develop skills kids need to do their work

train·ing (noun): the action of teaching a particular skill or type of behavior

As you read this step, consider:

1. The skills your kids have mastered and those that may be in need of additional development in order for them to take responsibility for their own Routines and work.

2. Ways in which you can provide formal and informal opportunities and experiences to develop those skills.

Overview

Day-to-day life is filled with development and Training opportunities, the focus of the fifth step.

Training provides kids with the essential skills they need to become Responsible, Resilient, and Resourceful leaders, able to manage their own work and to develop their own Routines. In addition to modeling and teaching the START Leadership language and processes, building training into everyday activities reinforces the leadership mindset, provides tools that can scaffold and build over time, provides opportunities to earn privileges, and builds self-assurance.

According to business, academic, and child development leaders, mastering a set of ten skills is essential for our kids to succeed in today's competitive and rapidly changing world. These skills can be refined by age and then practiced and reinforced at home with increasing sophistication over time.

The skills fall into the categories of Responsible, Resilient, and Resourceful, the Three Rs of Leadership.

Responsible: I know what to do and step up to do it.

1. Self-Direction: They see the big picture. They set appropriate goals, and they take initiative and ownership to do the work necessary to achieve them.

2. Ethics: They choose right over wrong — even when choosing right is harder and no one is watching.

3. Global Awareness: They understand the perspective of others who may have needs and views that are different from their own.

Resilient: I know why I'm the one to do it, and so stay with it, even when it's hard.

4. Grit: They recover from setbacks and they forge ahead. They are willing, eager, and able to take on worthwhile challenges even when it is hard.

5. EQ: Their social and emotional awareness and skills enable the productive management of themselves and their relationships.

6. Social Responsibility: They put their talents to work to make a difference in ways that are meaningful to their community and to them.

Resourceful: I know how to do it, and I know how to work with others to get it done.

7. Critical Thinking: They have the knowledge, skill, and discipline to conceptualize, analyze, and synthesize information that leads to meaningful and productive decision making and outcomes.

8. Creativity: They have the knowledge, skill, and discipline to apply original ideas to generate meaningful value.

9. Communication: They persuasively give and actively receive essential information.

10. Collaboration: They work with and leverage a group's talents to realize shared goals.

Even at the youngest ages, our kids benefit from experiencing the meaning and context of these skills and from putting them into practice. For example, a three-year-old learning to play well in the sand box, sharing toys, and taking turns is developing her skill in Global Awareness, while an 18-year-old is learning to understand the perspective of others in different communities, cultures, and countries.

Training opportunities can be woven into daily life. Games, projects, chores, and selected books and movies can be used to support the development of each of the essential leadership skills. Once established, the leadership language and processes developed through informal and formal training establish vocabulary that kids can use, build upon, and take with them as they move through school, college, and into the workplace and life as adults.

Create Training Opportunities

1. Assess Skills

Now and over time as your kids mature, assess the extent to which each skill is age-appropriately developed in your kids.

For each age, note which of the ten skills are:

N: Not Yet Evident

E: Emerging

D: Developing

M: Mastered

2. Track Skill Development

Document the assessments you make with respect to skills so that you can track improvement or spot areas for development over time.

Date _____

1. _____ Self Direction
2. _____ Ethics
3. _____ Global Awareness
4. _____ Grit
5. _____ EQ
6. _____ Social Responsibility
7. _____ Critical Thinking
8. _____ Creativity
9. _____ Communication
10. _____ Collaboration

3. Create Development Opportunities

Take action to create opportunities that foster the practice and development of skills that are not yet mastered.

As your kids age, continue to create opportunities for them to apply their skills in increasingly complex and sophisticated ways in order to scaffold and build their capabilities.

Coach and Champion their developing levels of mastery, and support them in their consistent use, including Routines, when possible.

Family Training Example

A START family shared this story of their son's college "internship" and his subsequent career opportunity. In the summer before his senior year, Michael elected to decline the competitive internships he was offered in favor of a job working construction in Mexico – where he could explore the people, the language, the culture, and the surfing, which was his passion.

In discussions with his parents, Michael made his case that as an adventurer at heart with a desire to expand his global awareness, self-direction, and grit, a summer in Mexico was ideally suited to meeting his goals. The experience would also give him a welcome break from the demands of his rigorous academic load – contributing to his greater sense of happiness and well-being.

Upon graduation, it was Michael's in-country experience in Mexico that gave him a competitive advantage in landing a plum position with a multinational consulting firm that was establishing a new practice in Mexico.

Training Case Study: The Challenges of Camp

This Training process was used to address a development gap with the 11-year-old son in a START family.

> "In a family of five, we have a lot going on every day. We've been thrilled to see the return on our time invested with the START process. Although it took some diligence and several months to get the hang of it, we had successfully selected our Tactics and developed a set of Routines that aligned with our Strategy. This was effective in streamlining our lives and in reducing the stress and tension of our mornings and evenings. And it helped us to create time for the things that are important to us individually and collectively.
>
> For the most part, our kids now know what they're doing, why they're doing it, and can figure out how to do it without requiring reminders and direction from us (i.e. nagging and micromanaging). But when the school year ended and the summer began, we were thrown out of our regular Routines and hit a few bumps in the transition.

In the spring, when we were making our summer plans, our middle son, Blake, chose a ten-week, adventure day camp for his activity. This aligned with his WIN Map, the family Resources, and our family Strategy: We value Family, Integrity, Courage, Teamwork, and Fun and choose actions and activities that develop RRR in order to raise kids who can lead well, be well, and do well.

The bump, or should I say, the opportunity for development, showed up in the second week of camp, when Blake took over the responsibility for packing what he'd need for the rotating activities at camp each day. I got a call at work that first Monday, asking if I could run home to get his rock climbing shoes and drop them off before lunch. On Wednesday, the second call requesting the delivery of his forgotten item went to my husband, who was working from home that day. His lack of responsibility was interfering with our ability to be responsible and productive at work.

Over the weekend, we encouraged Blake to establish a Routine, noting the positive impact that would have on all of us. He had been using a checklist he'd developed for camp, but we realized that since this was the first time he'd been to a camp where activities changed each day, he required some Training in order to manage well. He was lacking the critical thinking and self-direction skills required to manage a schedule that changed daily.

We worked with him (Coaching Leadership Style) to analyze the camp schedule, giving him opportunities to practice making decisions and to exercise self-direction in packing what he needed each night. He was able to master the skills and develop the Routine he needed to be Responsible for his own work. This proved to be an asset when he started middle school that fall, where changing classes required the critical thinking and self-direction skills he'd developed."

Lead Well, Do Well, Be Well

All kids are born with the capacity to engage, to innovate, and to lead. In our research and that of the scores of others, we find that the kids who fare best in preparedness and well-being have had opportunities to discover, practice, and develop their leadership skills and abilities in many areas over many years. They have at least one parent, teacher, or mentor who believes in them, who believes that happiness drives success, that leadership drives happiness, and that elements included in the START process drive leadership.

Intrinsically motivated and emotionally intelligent, the kids raised with this model demonstrate more meaningful, engaged behaviors at school, at home, and ultimately at work when compared to the extrinsically motivated kids for whom behaving, performing and achieving, and building a résumé for college admissions are the defining objectives. They develop leadership. They are the Responsible, Resilient, and Resourceful kids we hoped they would be. They have a deep sense of connection — to themselves, their work, and to how they matter in the world.

Given the opportunity, they can take the lead, in both small and large ways. When our kids' experiences are designed to build over time to provide increasing levels of responsibility and freedom, they have opportunities to apply the ways in which they're uniquely Wired, in areas in which they have strong Interest, to make a real difference where Needed in their family, their community, and the world. In this process, kids learn to believe in themselves. They experience broad success without sacrificing well-being.

And in so doing, as the Duke Professor promised they would, our kids develop the mindset and skills they need now to be happy, healthy, and successful.

START Now

The local and global challenges our kids will face in their lifetime will continue to escalate. By the time kids today graduate from high school, colleges will have changed their admissions criteria yet again. And by the time they graduate from college, technological shifts, recessions, and global dynamics will undoubtedly affect the employment opportunities of college grads. In the face of increasing uncertainty, we have the opportunity to give our kids a set of universal tools with which to face the future with confidence.

We can't wait.

The START tools presented here provide that set of universal tools. When our kids are with us at home, the family Strategy serves as a goal-driven, decision-making guide and an organizational framework. Corresponding Tactics evolve over time, as do parents' leadership styles, to meet evolving circumstances. Kids' Wiring and Interests emerge and shift over time to take advantage of opportunities and to meet needs they discover in their world. Periodic Assessment is essential. Routines become more sophisticated and shift in order to accomplish the evolving Tactics. Training becomes a smooth and integral part of daily life. Creating space for play, and reflection, and even boredom delivers significant benefits.

In the environment we create with this approach, kids thrive. In addition to all the positive opportunities for growth, they will also work hard, suffer disappointments and setbacks, be challenged socially and intellectually, and learn that they can bounce back, stronger and wiser.

Through it all, they will rely on us, their parents, to create a context of value and meaning, a lens through which they can understand the purpose of their work and see the connection to the outcomes they achieve. Their leadership experiences will equip them with the skills they need to lead their own lives well and to make a difference in the world, with and for others.

They will learn how to set their own Strategy, select their preferred Tactics, Assess their own progress, develop effective Routines, and seek Training to develop the skills that will allow them to do work that is meaningful and valued.

In the process, they will master the skills they need to maximize the opportunities they find while effectively navigating the inevitable challenges of life.

Responsible, Resilient, and Resourceful, they will Lead Well, Be Well, and Do Well in the lives they make for themselves.

We'd love to add your voice to this growing conversation. We invite you to share your thoughts, your experiences, and your stories with us.

(Twitter: @STARTLeader; Facebook: START Leadership).

For additional resources and to learn more about how you can START in your community, school, or workplace, visit START-Leadership.com.

BIBLIOGRAPHY

Research in Business
Emotional Intelligence by Daniel Goleman
Gallup StrengthsFinder 2.0 by Tom Rath
Good to Great by Jim Collins
The Happiness Advantage by Shawn Achor
Scaling Up Excellence by Bob Sutton and Huggy Rao
A Whole New Mind by Daniel Pink

Research in Education and Child Development
The Blessing of a Skinned Knee by Wendy Mogel
Creating Innovators by Tony Wagner
Doing School by Denise Pope
Mind in the Making by Ellen Galinsky
Mindset by Carol Dwek
The Nine Intelligences by Howard Gardner
The Price of Privilege by Madeline Levine

Wiring Resource Links
Gallup Organization: www.gallupstrengthscenter.com
Myers Briggs: www.myersbriggs.org/

CPSIA information can be obtained at www.ICGtesting.com
Printed in the USA
LVOW03s1927310715

448418LV00003B/14/P